THE BOOK OF URGENCY

CYNTHIA KNIGHT

THE BOOK OF URGENCY

Copyrights © 2024 Cynthia Knight

All rights reserved. No part of this book may be reproduced or transmitted in any form or by any means without written permission from the author.

ISBN 978-0-9852542-8-5

Author Disclaimer:

This book is the author's work. Any views or opinions represented or expressed in this book are personal and belong solely to the author. They do not represent the views of the author's current or past employers. Neither does it represent the views of people, institutions, or organizations that the author may associate with in a professional or personal capacity unless explicitly stated. Any views or opinions are not intended to malign any religion, ethnic group, club, organization, company, or individual.

Printed in the United States of America

Published in USA by Onyx Gavel Publishing
A subsidiary of Mosaic Consortium Group, LLC.

www.onyxgavel.com
publish@onyxgavel.com

DEDICATION

*This book is dedicated to everyone who actually believed me when I said I was writing this book. You are incredible people, because I didn't even believe myself when I said it.
Thank you for your support.*

P.S. This is probably the only funny thing you will read from this work. This is a heavy book.

CONTENTS

INTRODUCTION	1
SCRIPTURES	2
Urgent War Cry Part I	5
The Spiritual Paradigm Shift Matters	11
The Source Matters	31
Time Matters	49
Urgent War Cry Part-II	59
Special Section for BGLO & Secret Societies	65
NEW BOOK COMING SOON	72
END NOTES	73
REFERENCES	75

INTRODUCTION

This is an urgent call. This book goes against the grain for my personality. I strive to do things right and in order, according to standards/industry standards. I am a writer and a publisher and there are concrete rules and standards for both, but guess what? I serve a God who does not comply to man's standards and when God commands something, I need to get it done.

I have procrastinated for a variety of reasons, but not my will, God's will be done. God has the final say, without question. So, in an attempt to get this book out quickly this work may not have all the earmarking of an industry-standard book. It's okay, although I feel otherwise. I trust God and I'm taking the risk. The lack of editing and typos will not matter if the message is received in time to save someone. My idiosyncrasies and quirks (i.e. overthinking and perfectionism) are not to be entertained at this time. This is too important and too urgent of a message. There is not much time left.

You don't know me, but if you did, you would know, this is not me. I am not "that" person and have distinct opinions about some of "those" people. However, I guess God in his divine providence decided who better to use, than the one that wants no part of this, or to be grouped with "that" group.

I pray that the readers of this work take it back to God first. Do not trust me, trust God. Then if God approves, take it into your heart and heed the words. So, let's get to the meat of it, and it is meat, not milk. It is what it is...

May the Lord Bless you and protect you.
May the Lord Smile on You and be gracious to you.
May the Lord show you his favor
And give you his peace.

Numbers 6:24-26 (NLT)

~ Cynthia Knight

SCRIPTURES

Psalms 3:3

"But thou, O LORD, art a shield for me; my glory, and the lifter up of mine head."

Jeremiah 33:3

"Call unto me, and I will answer thee, and shew thee great and mighty things, which thou knowest not."

King James Version (KJV)

Urgent War Cry
Part I

Jesus loves each one of us. He loves us so much that he will provide every opportunity for us to self-reflect and self-correct, if necessary. God desires that none of us should be lost. This book was assigned to me and written in haste. It was not an assignment I felt comfortable with, but feelings are not facts. My feelings do not matter in this case, and my feelings will not deter the will of God.

Jesus Yeshua the Christ is continuing his appeal for the rescue and redemption of all souls across every platform. In the end, no person will stand before Him and say that they did not hear His call. The only explanation that will be given is that I heard the call of Jesus, Yeshua the Christ, and rejected His message.

God gave me the title *The Book of Urgency* and instructions to compile what He had revealed to me in a book. Urgent? I thought. I didn't feel like I had been given anything urgent. It was not until I began writing this book that it all came together. The order the book is currently in does not reflect the order in which it was given to me. The Holy Spirit gives me revelation in pieces, like pieces in a puzzle box. When God is ready, he takes those puzzle pieces and organizes them for me to see the full picture, blowing my mind each time it happens. This time is no different.

The spiritual realm or the spiritual atmosphere is shifting. The effects of the shift are seeping into the natural world and are being felt everywhere, even if people do not know or recognize what they are feeling. There is this palpable feeling of "something is about to happen" in both the spiritual and secular world. If I'm being honest, I see more secular* preaching going on in the streets than ever before. You see secular people posting mini-bible sermons that seem on point in their messaging,

> **Secular** - *not having any connection to religion.*
>
> **Worldly** - *relating to or consisting of physical and ordinary life rather than spiritual things*

but they are interlaced with profanity. The Culture has church cliché in their mouth. *"God is good, all the time," "Won't He do it".* Meanwhile the church is turning more worldly each day. The new year brought DJs, secular music, and dancing inside the church; alcoholic drinks at gospel concerts, Pastors suggesting to have weed sold at the church to attract new members, please "make this make sense"! What happened to "and do not be conformed to this world, but be transformed by the renewing of your mind, that you may prove what is that good and acceptable and perfect will of God Romans 12:2". God is not pleased. This is a critical moment in time.

God in his infinite grace and mercy is instructing his people to tell people what he is saying. God is using every day, ordinary people. The social media platforms are overrun with people sharing posts and videos detailing dreams, visions, prophecies, and posts of "God told me". Never in my wildest dreams did I expect to be one of those people, but here we are.

> **End Times** - *the period leading up to Judgment Day. All men will be judged for their actions during their time on earth.*
>
> **Last Days** - *a synonym for end times. The period before Jesus returns for those who believe in Him.*

Now my witness can be nothing more than my witness. I am not a Bible Scholar, Minister, or Theologian. I hold no title other than Child of God and Believer of Jesus, Yeshua the Christ. I can only tell you what has been revealed to me. I grew up in church, so I may naturally write "churchy" for the secular. For the church, I may write worldly to you because I use quite a few colloquial phrases. What is most important is that you hear what God is saying and I will try to present that the best way I can. For new believers or unbelievers, I will add context boxes to help with some of the church vernacular or terms that may be unfamiliar to those outside the church.

I manage people on my 9-5 and I can tell you after 31 years of experience, people are going to do exactly what they want to do. So, I'm not going out of my way to persuade, twist arms, or fire and brimstone anyone into anything. I am treating you exactly how I would want to be to be treated, and that is: 1) Give me all the information 2) Provide your references and receipts, and then 3) Let me make up my own mind. That's all I plan to do.

Story Time

When I was 11 years old, I saw two movies at church that would forever change my life. They were called a "Thief in the Night (1973)" and its sequel "A Distant Thunder (1978)". I viewed these in 1981. Both movies terrified me. They would leave an indelible mark on me and influence how I would make choices in my life for the foreseeable future. What I didn't know then, which I know now, is that movie was my introduction to the idea of being an end times warrior.

If I am being truthful, this is the absolute last thing I wanted for my life. These movies reinforced to me that I NEVER wanted to live during the end times. I didn't feel I was strong enough to endure during those times. They say if you want to make God laugh, tell him what you think. So fast forward to today, many would argue we are in the last days. I concur.

Writers are taught to use stories to connect, engage, and generate interest in their work. The rules of writing dictate I make myself relatable, so you will continue to read this work. However, this is not a conventional book. I am not a conventional writer, and this is not a conventional message. My goal for this work is to do my Father's bidding. I pray the reader hears, receives, understands, and decides. So, I'm just laying it out, straight information. It would behoove you to stick with it until the end. This book isn't something that has to do with you relating to me. I received an urgent message to pass on to you, so let's get straight to it.

The Spiritual Paradigm Shift Matters

We are experiencing a paradigm shift within the spirit realm. A paradigm shift is "an important change that happens when the usual way of thinking about or doing something is replaced by a new and different way"[1] With the pronouncement of the last days comes a myriad of spiritual atmospheric changes. The enemy has played the long game and strategically waited to release this unprecedented level of havoc, signaling the shift.

The world is experiencing pure evil and mindless chaos, the likes of which we have never seen before. Demonic worship, rituals, symbols, and sacrifice are now in the open. Nothing is hidden. The enemy is preparing to take possession of what he believes is his. The new norm includes idolatry, cabals, witches covens, bestiality, sacrileges, and abominations. All of this happens openly and is accepted by people. Society is being groomed for the new world order.

It has never been as important as it is now for those in Christ to know who they are and whose they are. We must remember God has dominion over everything, but he has given dominion to man as well *"God made man to have dominion over the works of His hands and put all things under his feet"* Psalm 8:6.

You would think and hope that while this evil escalation was happening, the church would rise to the challenge in a united mass movement. Regrettably, that is not the case. As the Bible foretold, there has been a great falling away. Parishioners are leaving the church in exponential numbers or have not returned since the Covid lockdowns. Covid brought on the deaths of many prominent Church Leaders. Leaving many ministries uncovered and inept to deal with the principalities and spiritual

> "**Principalities** and powers in the Bible are levels of demons or the presence of demonic activity. These beings are real, and their primary goal is to kill, injure, worry, destroy, vex, harass, irritate, confuse, frustrate, and bother humans."
>
> **Intercessor-** "The definition is basic: an intercessor is someone who prays, petitions or begs God in favor of another person. It's a Biblical concept that appears often".

warfare attacking their areas.

All types of spirits have infiltrated the church, and there are only a few true and effective deliverance ministries. The intercessors of old have died off without teaching the new generation how to hold their ground and territory and protect the veil that separates us from the evil realm. Meanwhile, the Body of Christ and gospel music continue to conform to the ways of this world, further weakening our stance. The Bible said this would happen, and it has. God is not pleased.

> *But know this, that in the last days perilous times will come: For men will be lovers of themselves, lovers of money, boasters, proud, blasphemers, disobedient to parents, unthankful, unholy, unloving, unforgiving, slanderers, without self-control, brutal, despisers of good, traitors, headstrong, haughty, lovers of pleasure rather than lovers of God, having a form of godliness but denying its power. And from such people turn away! 2 Timothy 3:1-5*

The current shaking of the church may come with devastating and soul damaging effects. Currently, at this writing, there is an enormous scandal surrounding a prominent church leader. People all over the world and in political circles know this leader.

At the time of this writing, it has not been determined whether the allegations are true or false. The truth is, regardless of the outcome- allegations true or allegations false, the Body of Christ has suffered a major black eye. The fallout is astounding. Social media is in a frenzy, providing endless material for content creators. Everyone has an opinion. Secular people are harshly judging the church and using this scandal to hold on to and justify their current lifestyle choices. They argue that it's better to remain in the world than to be deceived by false pastors and prophets in the church.

But don't lose hope. God is raising a remnant, but this will be a fight like we have never experienced. While the Body of Christ was slacking, the enemy was preparing. The spiritual wickedness in high places has been preparing for this battle. The good news is we already know how this story ends...God wins. Now you wouldn't want to go through all of this for God to say depart from me, I know you not.

> *"Not everyone who says to Me, 'Lord, Lord,' shall enter the kingdom of heaven, but he who does the will of My Father in heaven. Many will say to Me in that day, 'Lord, Lord, have we not prophesied in Your name, cast out demons in Your name, and done many wonders in Your name?' And then I will declare to them, 'I never knew you; depart from Me, you who practice lawlessness!"*
> Matthew 7:21

Sign of the Times

Time is of the essence has never been a truer statement than it is today. The countdown to the "unknown" is happening, and it has never been more palpable. Believers in Jesus Christ define this period as the precursor of events outlined in the Bible before the return of Christ. People outside the belief system of the return of Christ, and those with a secular worldview, blame symptoms: the economy, war, crime, global warming, and social decline. One thing is for certain, everyone can feel it, no matter what they ascribe as a meaning for it. Because few people know how to effectively or properly describe the "feeling," they reduce it to the tired cliché of "time is short".

As a Believer in Jesus Christ, striving to meet him in eternity, I believe what the Bible states. The Bible tells us all these signs and symptoms are the signs of the times before Jesus's long-awaited and holy return. For the naysayers that contend religious people have been saying time is short and God is returning for centuries; I contend you do not understand time or God in time, but we will get into that later.

Everyone can feel this paradigm shift, church and secular alike. They may not be able to explain what they are feeling, but church and secular people know something is off in the world and something is coming. The earth is screaming. We have rain and floods in the desert. Birds are gathering in large populations and sitting by the hundreds in odd places. Fish, sharks, and whales are beaching themselves or we find them in waters they should not dwell. Rivers that are thousands of years old are now drying up, just as the Bible foretold. However, the church isn't preaching on it.

Signs of the Times	Where in the Bible
Euphrates River drying up	Revelations 16:12
Earthquakes	Luke 21:11; Matthew 24:7
Parents and children murdering each other	Mark 13:12
Wars	Matthew 24:6
Political Corruption	Isaiah 1:4
Church Corruption	Mathew 24:10-12
False Prophets	Matthew 7:15; 2 Peter 2-3
Social Media Addiction/Self-Absorption	2 Timothy 3: 2-9
Defiling the Church	1 Corinthians 3:17
Hateful People	2 Timothy 3:1-5
Sexual Perversions	1 Corinthians 5:13

Through social media, the secular world is getting the word out about these unusual activities. Shamefully and ironically, the secular world is churching more than the church in some respects. They are expressing and unveiling the happenings within the church and their severe disappointment in the church. At times the secular world seems to know right from wrong better than the church. The mere fact that everything is upside down brings Isaiah 5:20 to life *"They say that what is right is wrong and what is wrong is right; that black is white and white is black; bitter is sweet and sweet is bitter."* The church prophets and sign of the times observers are crying out on social media. God is using everyone to get his Word out. Which confirms that time is short.

I came across a TikTok post. Before seeing this post, I was not aware of this lady, or her political or organizational affiliations, but I thought her breakdown of the world's climate was an eye-opening assessment of where she sees the world at this moment in time. It aligns with the urgent nature of this work. If this is going on in the world, what is going on in the spirit? *Disclaimer: I do not follow this lady or know anything else about her other than this post. This is not the entire speech, just an excerpt:*

"The final goal is to eradicate humanity as we know it. Once you understand the final destination it becomes much easier to look back and identify the psychological conditioning, the biological tampering, the cultural grooming, and the educational prepping that we have been subjected to for decades in preparation to making us accept a post-human future.

It takes a lot of physical and psychological abuse to get an intelligent species like ours to agree to its own extinction. Most, if not all, that has transcended in the last 60 years was designed to get us closer to accepting such a dystopian reality. Whether you care to accept it or not, we live in a hyper-controlled matrix. Where our perception of reality is meticulously planned, managed, and executed, in order to control and steer us in whichever direction they wish, and the direction is a post-human world.

For this, they first needed to destabilize, dehumanize, and demoralize humanity through every means possible. The destruction of the nuclear family, children being indoctrinated by the state, abortion, the eradication of God and spirituality from education, life in mega-cities and away from nature, toxic food, air and water, social media replacing real human connection and interaction, engineered financial crisis and taxation, endless wars, and massive migration.

Stress, anxiety, depression, drugs and alcohol, constant fearmongering, moral relativism as the new religion, and I could go on and on about how humanity is being influenced and forced to move away from all the things that give us strength, security, purpose, and meaning...~Laura Aboli UnifydGlobal[2].

Selah.

DJ's in the Pulpits

Some Pastors, Gospel Artists, and Gospel Artists turned preachers are defiling the church temple with secular music integration. Again, I say some, not all. However, it is now becoming more of the norm for pastors to allow dancing and secular music inside the church, not the church hall, the sanctuary. They argue the church is too spiritual and legalistic. I understand the context of the argument. However, we are going from the one extreme of cultish legalism to sanctified defilement. Changing the church to look like the world is not the answer.

God asked for one day to be devoted to rest and for that day to be kept holy. Introducing secular music inside the church is defilement, similar to bringing an unworthy sacrifice inside the temple. In the Old Testament, if the sacrifice was not acceptable, the priest would die. He had to wear bells at the hem of his garment as he entered the Holy of Holies so the people on the other side could track his movements by the sound of the bells to know the sacrifice was acceptable, and the priest was still alive. Secular music inside the church sanctuary is a defilement and an unworthy offering to God.

Now that the demonic activity conducted within the record industry is coming to light and we are learning more about the satanic practice of, praying over the music, invoking demonic spirits to seduce the listener to increase record and streaming sales. Why would you bring that into the sanctuary? This type of behavior demonstrates that we do not know or recognize our enemy. If you would like to learn more about this topic, I discuss it in Red Pill Revelations: Know Your Enemy.

> *"Don't overlook the obvious here, friends. With God, one day is as good as a thousand years, a thousand years as a day. God isn't late with his promise as some measure lateness. He is restraining himself on account of you, holding back the End because he doesn't want anyone lost. He's giving everyone space and time to change." 2 Peter 3: 8-9 MSG*

This book is written to tell you the Lord is not pleased. He is angry, but He is still trying to provide everyone with an opportunity to repent. Repent means to turn away. God wants everyone to turn away from evil and be with Him. You must choose a side before you run out of time.

False Prophets, Apostasy Deception

The enemy has infiltrated every area of the world, including the church. The Bible warns us of false prophets. Social media encourages and promotes self-centered and self-aggrandizement. The constant need to be seen and receive validation and promotion through "likes", has been fertile ground for seeds of deception through the use of false prophets. This social media world has created a false prophet called "The Culture". The Culture dictates to and controls the mob. The mob shows up in a variety of ways, court of public opinion, fan hives surrounding a celebrity, politics, and religion. Apostasy is running rampant in the church.

"Apostasy is the turning away from God in rebellion or apathy. God's people must beware of inward rebelliousness as much as the outward wickedness that manifests such rebellion."[3] The Bible has warned us multiple times that the Body of Christ would come against this rebellion.

> **Apostasy** - <u>an act of refusing to continue to follow, obey, or recognize a religious faith: abandonment of a previous loyalty</u>

> *Take care, brothers, lest there be in any of you an evil, unbelieving heart, leading you to fall away from the living God. But exhort one another every day, as long as it is called "today," that none of you may be hardened by the deceitfulness of sin. For we have come to share in Christ, if indeed we hold our original confidence firm to the end. As it is said, "Today, if you hear his voice, do not harden your hearts as in the rebellion." Hebrews 3:12-15 and*
>
> *You therefore, beloved, knowing this beforehand, take care that you are not carried away with the error of lawless people and lose your own stability. But grow in the grace and knowledge of our Lord and Savior Jesus Christ. To him be the glory both now and to the day of eternity. Amen. 2 Peter 3:17–18 (ESV)*

We received a warning that this could become a permanent state in the last days. "The possibility of permanent apostasy seems suggested by Hebrews 6: 4–6, though the wider context of Hebrews 6 suggests the underlying issue is continued rebellion against God and hard-hearted opposition to the gospel—not that the people cannot turn from their apostasy but that, like Israel, they refuse to return."[4]

> *For it is impossible, in the case of those who have once been enlightened, who have tasted the heavenly gift, and have shared in the Holy Spirit, and have tasted the goodness of the word of God and the powers of the age to come, and then have fallen away, to restore them again to repentance, since they are crucifying once again the Son of God to their own harm and holding him up to contempt. Hebrews 6:4–6 (ESV)*

Another problem in "the culture" society is people like to repeat (steal) what others have posted just for the sake of likes. This becomes a problem with prophecy and Christians using the social media platforms to warn people. It's like the game telephone. The message starts one way, but by the time it gets to the last person, it's an entirely different message. The internet is free. You can be anyone you want to be. You can be a prophet on Monday and a pimp on Tuesday. It is critically important to test the spirits.

Everyone's discernment will be tested in these last days and people will be fooled. The elect will be fooled. Pray to God to cover your mind and fortify your spirit so that you do not get fooled. I hear so many people say they pray for discernment, and that is good. However, in addition to discernment ask God for revelation. Ask Him to reveal anything that can be standing in between you and Him, request that he make that known to you.

The days we are in and heading into will require you to know God, know his character, and discern his ways. Hold his hand and walk and talk with him now, while He is yet to be found. You will need to strengthen yourself to be strong enough and confident enough to know God's ways, just in case God gets quiet.

Engaging with God, receiving a Word from God, Confirmation, Signs and Wonders have become so familiar to us we overlook the period of 400 years when God remained silent. We assume and take for granted that God will continue to operate in the manner in which He has dealt with His People. We know God will never leave us or forsake us, but that does not mean He may not be silent. Therefore, it is so important to praise and worship God for engaging with us, and for letting us feel and experience his presence. It is a gift.

The constant reliance on social media for information about God opens the door to deception. We are living in an age of mass deception. Politics, Entertainment, and the Media have perfected the art of deception. You have to fight hard to find the truth each day. You constantly have to take double and triple looks at pictures to make sure they are not photoshopped or created by AI. Foreign countries have infiltrated

American platforms with "fake news" to distort news and create chaos. The Culture lies in wait, just anticipating the next misstep, verbal or otherwise, so they can pounce. The Culture's language is clichés, new and old. So, because you are seeing and hearing the same thing repeatedly, the culture dictates that as truth.

Attack on the Truth

The United States is a small microcosm of the world. The search for truth is a real thing. History and facts are becoming outdated concepts. The common phrase "My Truth" places a person's truth over the actual truth. "I'm telling My truth "Is the catchphrase, however, most are not interested in your truth, just THE truth. God is the Truth. *"Jesus saith unto him, I am the way, the truth, and the life: no man cometh unto the Father, but by me. John 14:6"*

We have cultures and subcultures. Truth is subjective and no longer definitive. There are variants and sub-variants. Each day brings its own trouble. So, at some point, you realize that everything you've learned is a misnomer, fallacy, half-truth, or simply a lie. Truth is a rare commodity like water in a desert. The only place to get 100% truth is from God. He is the truth.

What makes matters worse is we are a nation of people who love lies. Humanity claims it want the truth, but in reality, we want, and in some ways, need the lies. Lies and fallacies allow us to live exactly how we want, with no accountability.

Culturally, we begin the indoctrination of lies during the early childhood development years and it continues throughout of lives. We then grow up and continue to perpetuate the same lies told to us, so the cycle continues for generations. I do a deep dive into fantasy and holiday lies in <u>Red Pill Revelations: Know Your Enemy</u>. Have you ever considered why we need to keep this cycle of these lies going? Are we happier with lies or has it become so convoluted that we can no longer tell the lies from the truth? Or the degree to which they are tearing down society?

Satan was able to cause the fall of man simply by stating a lie. He made a statement, did not provide proof, evidence, or context, and from that false statement, he altered the destiny of Man in the Garden. This methodology of just stating a lie and standing firm on it is still used today. Politics has adopted it as its tactic of choice.

This blatant type of lying is another example of Satan mocking God. God, being Almighty and Sovereign, speaks things into existence. He spoke a word and from nothingness and dust created both the world and man. Satan cannot create anything. He is an imitator, not a creator. Satan is the father of lies and the truth is not in him. He mocks God by saying false things, false doctrines, and lies to defile and destroy man.

God is God. There is no other like him. Therefore, just because you say it, doesn't make it true or truth. Man, nor Satan, can create in the manner God did during the creation. However, man is made in the image of God, and we can utilize faith and make pronouncements with our mouths, which allows God to use our words to bring forth the things that we speak. You start this spiritual process with your mouth, so the words you speak have importance and can be used for good or bad purposes.

Satan can use our words against us, "death and life are in the power of the tongue, and those who love it will eat its fruits. Proverbs 18:21 (ESV). Satan is the accuser of men. The Bible described the serpent as the most intelligent creature created. So, the enemy is intelligent and cunning. He knows God's word and waits for opportunities to conjure confusion. Once your tongue goes rogue and speaks outside of God's word, the enemy is right there to take those words back to God and accuse man in hopes of bringing that negative thing to fruition in your life. That's why it's so important to watch what you say. Blessings and curses come from the same place, your mouth.

God's word cannot return to him void and the devil uses this truth to manipulate and conjure negative faith. I was listening to a content creator on TikTok and he called it demonic prophecy and explained it in a really clear and concise way. Below are excerpts of what he said:

"I like to call it demonic prophecy. You see, there's a theme that happens in the world. Where movies or shows or things are put out. And then those things seem to come to pass... "Many people might tell you, oh, it's because of the secret rule of the world. They have to admit to you with their karmic retribution. They have to admit what they're doing so that way they can do it.... That's not how this works. You see this? Is called demonic prophecy and it works quite the opposite. Of what you think.

Let me explain it to you so that way you understand, and you can stop participating in demonic prophecy. You see all authority on heaven and on Earth has been given unto Jesus...He gave that authority unto you...He Jesus gave all of the authority that he took back from the devil unto you.

So yes, even though satan rules the world, the authority has been restored. Your academic authority has been given back to us, if we use it, but if we use it improperly satan and the demons can influence that authority for their benefit... When you speak things, you are accessing a prophetic nature that the Lord has given unto you. And that prophetic nature is the ability to speak things into existence. Satan knows this. The demons know this and because of their defeat, they can only get you to speak to prophecy the negative things of the world. So that the demon horde that surrounds it can make the statement. "The Prophet said it we can do. It now".

So there is a horde of demons waiting for your negative words to be spoken so that they can take effect. And they say, Lord Lord, your prophet said that these terrible things will happen. Your prophet said that that the cars will be hacked the waterways will be poisoned. Your prophets said this, so we can do it. We have the right to do it, Lord, your Prophet said it.

The demons are waiting for you to speak these terrible things into existence. And it's really getting irritating when I see these movies come out and everybody continues to speak this fear into society. That's what the demons want because they want the fear to be perpetuated over, and over and over and over and over. Until the prophets begin to speak it. And when you speak it. You are granting the demonic realm the authority to carry it out. This is demonic prophecy.... Stop being demonically influenced, prophets of God. Stop allowing the fear to affect you. We walk by faith, not by sight. This is how the process works. It is a spiritual battle. You are battling with a spiritual realm. Your words are powerful".
~@DemonErasers & @Beauty_from_ashes7 [5]

God is using this moment in time to allow the truth to come out, even though it is being attacked. This is a battle with a spiritual realm.

> *For we wrestle not against flesh and blood, but against principalities, against powers, against the rulers of the darkness of this world, against spiritual wickedness in high places. Ephesians 6:12.*

The elaborate nature of the lies and the level of deception are undergirded and held in place by rituals, spells, and spiritual wickedness that one could not conceive. You must protect your mind. Jesus and the Holy Spirit must live inside of you to protect you in these evil days. I'm reminded of a scene from the movie *Left Behind: World at War*, which was adapted from the book *Nicolae*, the third book of the Left Behind series by Jerry Jenkins and Tim LaHaye.

In one scene, a reporter had just accepted Jesus into his heart before a meeting he was attending to witness and report on with United Nations Leaders. During the meeting, the Antichrist murdered a man in front of the entire group, including the reporter. After the murder, the Antichrist casts a spell over the room and states a different version of events than what happened. He told all the people in the room to report what he had just said to the police when they arrived. The spell worked on everyone, and they repeated verbatim what the Antichrist had spoken to them. Everyone except the reporter was under the spell. Because he had accepted Jesus into his heart as his personal Savior and was covered by the blood of Jesus, he saw the murder and was not affected by the spell. It was a powerful scene that left a lasting impression on me. This type of protection is open to anyone who will accept it, and the spiritual battle we confront is more severe than what any movie can depict.

Co-Mingling

During my quiet time with God, I experienced another revelation, specifically about co-mingling. To co-mingle is "to mix together things of different types".[6] God warned Solomon not to intermarry with the females of the foreign lands because they worshipped other gods. Solomon did not listen and married many of these women because their beauty seduced him and thus, he mangled the blood of Israel with pagan gods. This resulted in apostasy for Solomon in his old age and his following Ashtoreth and Milcom. In addition, Solomon constructed shrines for his foreign wives to burn incense and sacrifice to their gods, Chemosh, Molech, a wicked thing in the eyes of the one true God (1 Kings 11:4-8).

Fast forward to today, the body of Christ has also received warnings/advice not to mix with the ways of the world. But yet and still we ponder about the fall of the church. Could it be because of a similar type of co-mingling? The modern-day church has adopted many of the secular ways and standards of the world that keep them distanced from the unadulterated Word of God. Looking at church clips on social media, it is very difficult to tell or separate a secular person from a Christian person. Pastor's robes have been replaced with designer outfits or athletic wear. I'm not a traditionalist and I'm not legalistic, but a lack of decorum has spilled into the church. There is nothing to tell the church apart from the world. We co-sign this co-mingling because, for some of us, the church is boring, and we grew up in an overbearing legalistic church environment. I get it. It's nice to walk into church and hear a beat, not have to buy different clothes, just be. This is serving your flesh.

The same is true of gospel music. Many gospel artists attend secular music award shows and work with secular artists. Many of these award shows contain demonic ritualistic ceremonies. A person representing Christ should have a problem with being in that environment. I have not seen one Instagram or TikTok with a Gospel artist claiming to have converted a secular artist at an award show. This loosening of the belt has made the pants fall down on the church. The problem with this type of co-mingling is much of the secular music that is sampled for use by gospel music has been prayed over ritualistically by witches and sorcerers to enhance record sales when it was a secular song.

So now you take that defiled music sample and insert it into a gospel song. It defiles the anointing. Then we wonder why we don't possess the same strength and power and can't perform miracles or healings as in the days of old. There is no need to ponder. The answer is the Body of Christ has defiled itself with commingling. It is a spiritual thing, not a flesh thing.

The Church Has COVID

Let's put co-mingling in a way I know everyone will understand. The best way to describe this is to say the Body of Christ has COVID. I know this sounds strange, but indulge me, and allow me to break this down for you. I'm not talking about the literal Covid virus. I'm talking about a spiritual realm manifestation with all the attributes of the natural world Coronavirus.

When Covid emerged, it captured the entire world and held it hostage. The authorities advised us to isolate, wear masks, and practice social distancing by staying at least six feet away from any person when in public. If you did not abide by this guidance, we were told we were putting ourselves at substantial risk of catching COVID. When this all began, we were dealing with a deadly variant of COVID for which our natural bodies had no effective defense. Scientists had not developed vaccines during this period. So, the world went into lockdown. Whoever you were with, you were told to isolate and quarantine with those people. The imminent danger was in proximity. Being too close could cost you your life.

The revelation given to me was the body of Christ has a similar spiritual COVID for lack of a better word. So, it is in the natural, so it is in the spiritual. Let's flesh this out. The problem with COVID is it is an ever-changing virus with an untold number of variants. Each time we think we have it under control, another variant emerges. Each variant brings its own symptoms, side effects, and biological responses by individuals. So, when I say the Body of Christ has COVID, I'm trying to explain a concept using an example every person on the planet should understand.

God has instructed that the Body of Christ to be separate, set apart, and peculiar. Throughout time, man has fought against that distinction. We see this in the previous example of Solomon when God instructed him not to intermarry with the Pagan women. Although they were beautiful, they contained a contagious connection to the demonic realm through their customs, practices, and worship of false gods. Solomon was seduced and enchanted, not only by beauty, but by proximity. So even back then, we saw being too close to something can lead to infection.

The body of Christ has positioned itself in a precarious spiritual situation by being so close to the secular. It has opened and exposed itself to the possibility of infection, possession, and defilement. We have adopted "the cultures" perspective that God welcomes everything and everyone without rebuke. This is not true and it is a false doctrine. God welcomes everyone who will repent of their ways that are not like him.

What does it mean to repent? It means to turn away from and go another way. This can be interpreted as recognizing a thing and putting more space between you and it, so you are not infected and consumed by the ways of the world. Now I know that sounds very churchy, but God has given us a real-life example in COVID-19. If you are too close to someone with COVID-19, there is a high probability you will come down with COVID-19. Each time you recover, you are still at risk for another variant of COVID-19 and each variant brings with it its own experience. Each person reacts differently to COVID-19. One individual may die. One individual may suffer symptoms and be very ill but can recover. Other individuals may suffer from the phenomenon called long COVID-19. Long COVID has been known to have significant respiratory, neurological, and cardiovascular effects for those afflicted with this more serious complication of COVID-19.

That's the natural side. Let's translate that into the spiritual realm. Each time you come within proximity to the demonic realm, you are putting yourself at spiritual risk of being infected, possibly perverted, or maybe even consumed. You risk encountering spiritual warfare that you are unprepared for or have encountered prematurely. You never want to put your spiritual gift at risk of being afflicted with long-term COVID-19 in the spiritual realm. That may have significant negative effects on your ability to stand against the devil's schemes.

So, I hear someone out there saying, well eventually you get healed. To which I counter, do you? As of now, scientists have not discovered a cure for COVID-19, and individuals who were infected develop antibodies in their blood, indicating their past infection. Not to mention the different variants associated with reinfection. Same in the spiritual world. Think of variants as another demonic entity. Now I don't know about you, but I don't want any spiritual residue or antibodies showing any connection to the demonic realm. You can repent and turn away from one demonic entity, but if you turn back, you can come away with demonic exposure seven times worse. Then it goes and brings along with it seven other spirits more wicked than itself, and they come in and live there, and the last condition of that person becomes worse than the first. That is the way it will also be with this evil generation. [7]

When you successfully fight off one variant/demonic attack, you are subject to another variant or demonic attack if you place yourself in proximity. We are on another level. There has been a shift. The complication to this new level, and possibly the most dangerous in this scenario, is the asymptomatic carrier. The person who has come in close contact and carries the virus but shows no appearance or symptoms of the virus.

The modern-day church is the asymptomatic carrier when it locks arms with the secular world. Spiritually, we become the asymptomatic carrier walking around with no symptoms, exposing babes in Christ and unbelievers to demonic influence for which they have no spiritual ability to fight. The babes in Christ mimic the seasoned Christians. So, if the gospel artist who exclusively sang gospel is now changing their public walk with God. What does that say? Were you lying before pretending to be holy or are you lying now? It sullies the Body of Christ all due to its proximity to the secular music industry.

As in Solomon's case, how long can you be around a thing before you slowly, not all at once, start compromising by letting your standards down? This is ok, and that is ok. I can go here with them. I can go there with them. Then one day, you wake up from this type of activity and realize that you have become contaminated and have spiritual COVID. The dangerous part is you may be held responsible for being an asymptomatic carrier if it results in the downfall of an unknowing believer.

The devil doesn't care how he takes you down. It can be subtle, or it can be big, as long as you go down. The devil is an accuser of men, and he will not relent. So, if you are unknowingly walking around with spiritual perversion and spiritual idolatry that you just caught because of proximity at a major artist concert. That artist had been conjuring demonic spirits before the show and used his/her voice to seduce the crowd. Are you not infected? Fast forward to you standing before the King of Kings to be judged, and He says "I know you not" because of infections you are unaware of, mainly because of demonic influence. How does that work? Show me Bible for this... I am glad you asked:

> *"For the time is coming when people will not endure sound teaching, but having itching ears they will accumulate for themselves teachers to suit their own passions, and will turn away from listening to the truth and wander off into myths. 2 Timothy 4:3-4*
>
> *Be sober-minded; be watchful. Your adversary, the devil, prowls around like a roaring lion, seeking someone to devour. Resist him, firm in your faith, knowing that the same kinds of suffering are being experienced by your brotherhood throughout the world. 1 Peter 5:8-9 ESV*

So, it is imperative that we put on the whole armor to protect ourselves from fiery darts that may come to us by way of proximity, which can lead to spiritual contamination. I can't emphasize enough the importance of being mindful of where you assemble and who you assemble with, as you will be held accountable.

Jackie Hill Perry will take this section out with her words of wisdom. Those who have an ear to hear please hear what is being said to the church and about the church:

> *"The church has been insane. Absolutely insane. I don't even have to say it. We've seen 15,000 Tik-Toks at this point about everything that's going on and happening in the church. what I'm here to say is guard your heart from hopelessness.*
>
> *Because what can happen when you see carnality being sanctified; when you see pulpits made common instead of sacred. When you see false prophets among God's people functioning in the spirit of divination, instead of the spirit of God. Saying true things but living bad lives. When you see the Bible being mishandled and abused for selfish ambition and gain. Like, like when you see prosperity teaching being packaged as your purpose and dah, dah, dah, independent of what God and His word has said...like when you see that type of stuff it is,*

discouraging; and you start to, you start to wonder; if righteousness is real. If holiness is possible. If faithfulness is even a thing anymore. And so you start to doubt, subtly, and in very small ways God, and his word. And that's when the enemy sneaks in, and that's when he starts to get access to you. When you start to move in the same way they do because you laid aside your hope. You get what I'm saying? Like so guard your heart from that. Like because either the grave is empty or isn't.

Like the Bible warned us about this stuff. They said it will always be wheat among tears. That there will be false teachers among us. That there will, there will be, wolves in sheep's clothing. That there will be people who have a form of Godliness but deny its power. They told us that. But you know what they also told us? You know what Paul told Timothy? He said but as for you- preach the word-

You know what Jude told the people he was writing to? He said, but you beloved, you make sure that you abide in God's love. Like the epistles also told us what to do in the midst of the foolishness, right, which is keep your eyes on Jesus. For he is the founder and perfecter of your faith.

In Philippians he says the work that he started in the real church, he will finish. At the end of Jude, he says to him who was able to keep us from stumbling; and to present us faultless and blameless, before his glorious presence with great joy. God, is supreme- Jesus is King- and He is Lord- and trust me, He will not be mocked. He will not be mocked. You could use his name and do whatever you want to do, in the meantime, you can be a functional atheist, you could you could do that if you want, but He won't be mocked. But in the meantime church, if you love Jesus, keep looking at Jesus. More than you even look at what's happening in the church. Don't let it distract you from what He's called you to do in the earth. OK! Alright. ~Jackie Hill Perry(@jackiehillperryduh)⁸

The Source Matters

Night is Coming

I perceive irony as life's joke, and although I have the heart of a fighter, I lack the physique of an athlete. Nonetheless, my spirit remains that of a fighter. My friends tease and laugh about how harmless I look and sound. I have a high-pitched and soft-spoken voice, which is deceptive. They call me a sleeper. I'm nice until I'm not. God is still working on me. Pray for me.

Just like my inner man does not look like or have the characteristics of my outer man, the same dichotomy exists in the spirit realm. Let's look at a couple of examples from the movies to illustrate my point. In the movie The Matrix, we see a similar dichotomy. While the characters are on the ship the Nebuchadnezzar, they wear tattered clothes and look impoverished. However, inside the matrix, they are impeccably dressed. They can do incredible things with their "freed" minds inside the matrix. They are called to save others.

Here's another example, in the movie Avatar, the main character Jake Sully is a paraplegic due to his war injuries. He was frail and had suffered extreme loss of muscle mass from sitting in his wheelchair. Avatar is a futuristic picture so there was a machine that could transport Jake to another dimension. Jake was a giant in this realm, powerful, in perfect physical condition, and a masterful warrior. Jake's natural physical body was not a representation of the powerful warrior living inside him in the other dimension. Jake was called to be a warrior and saved the inhabitants in that other dimension, despite his physical condition in the natural world.

God showed me the same type of scenario is going on now. There are powerful spiritual warriors for God in the spirit realm. You can't tell by looking at your physical, but God knows, and he is calling out to you. You've been laying low, waiting for a signal. The signs are pointing to the fact the time is now.

On the other side, the enemy copies God. He has created big and scary illusions to deter us from entering this fight. To understand and operate in or around the spirit realm requires discernment, complete self-awareness, and a close and intimate relationship with Yeshua/Jesus Christ. Now I don't know what position you are called to, only you and God know that. However, we are all called to be ready with clean armor.

As we enter this Jewish year of 5784, there is still a lot of work for the Body of Christ, the Church, to do. The enemy has elevated his game and his tactics, besides the fact that he is no longer hiding. We are witnessing Satan and his demonic realm being worshipped in plain sight out in the open. They are luring our children, family, and friends with tactics we have never seen before.

We hear people always saying things like "the devil", "the enemy", "the enemy is at work". What exactly does that mean? We get mad and frustrated when bad things happen in our lives. The Culture would have us believe, that if we wake up and say affirmations, if we are positive, and have positive thoughts, then we are good and effective people. For those who lean into faith a little more, they may add a little morning and evening prayer as an attempt to stave off the enemy. This is not going to cut it. The Body of Christ is being called to operate differently.

However, in times of REAL trouble, when we are facing a situation that requires immediate intervention by God, we often feel defeated because we don't know how to pray and effectively speak to the situation at hand. Those brief morning and evening prayers are ineffective in a difficult situation and often have us posting on social media asking for prayers from the "prayer warriors".

Prayer Warriors, sometimes called intercessors, are those persons who are in a direct and constant prayer relationship with God. Because of this relationship, Prayer Warriors/Intercessors have immediate access to get a prayer through to God and move God with their prayers to act on behalf of a person or situation.

The unknown truth is we all can be prayer warriors! This ability is available to anyone through prayer and relationship with God. We are ineffective in prayer and spiritual warfare because we do not truly know our enemy and the destruction, he intends for us. We do not know and understand our spiritual selves and the power that can be contained within us, and we are not properly wearing our armor or interacting with our Sovereign General, God. The war is shifting and the way we will be required to fight is different. It is imperative to know how to fight, even if the new fight is to stand.

The Bible shows us instances where the disciples (followers of Jesus) could not cast out demons or be effective with deliverance. The same is happening today. As we move forward in time, it is more critical than ever that we return to our former strength, as the Body of Christ. John 9:4 states, "While it's daytime, we must do the works of him who sent me. Night is coming when no one can work". Theologians debate what "Night" means in this scripture. Night can mean death. It may mean the judgments that are mentioned in Revelations, the Rapture, or a whole host of things.

I am a literal person. I interpret things exactly as they are said. So, for me, the literal one, "night" means the absence of light, the opposite of day. The very next verse supports my interpretation because Jesus says, "While I am in the world, I am the light of the world". Therefore, let's decipher "night is coming" to mean there is a time when God will remove himself from this world, giving full reign to the powers of the air, which will yield darkness to man. Let me break it down.

In the bible days, to have light at night, you used fire or lamps with oil. We read about the virgins being forewarned to have oil for their lamps because the bridegroom was coming. Making this scripture relevant to today, when I need light at night, my light comes from a lamp that is plugged into an electrical socket. Without an electricity source, my lamp will not work, and I will be in the dark.

Let's go a little deeper. If I take that same lamp across the pond to Great Britain, the lamp still will not work because the electricity source in Great Britain is not formatted for it. Electrical outlets in Great Britain are not the correct power source for my American lamp, without the proper adapter. So not only must I have the correct power source to obtain my light; I must also have the correct adapter. Then and only then will my lamp work. It's all about the correct power source.

The eminent danger of darkness looms when the United States, Russia, China, North Korea, and Iran clash. There is constant chatter and threat of attacks targeting the power grid. This type of attack would bring chaos and immediate terror, as it plunges any nation into total darkness. Water production depends on electricity. Hospitals and operating rooms depend on electricity. Traffic signals, prison security, airlines, all communication, and all employment depend on electricity. The loss of light and power creates a doomsday scenario.

There is a phrase in Christian vernacular that states "So it is in the natural, so it is in the spiritual." Night is coming, and I want to make sure you are plugged into the correct power source (God) to receive your light (Eternity with Him).

Source Switching- The Root of the Matter

Source switching is a tactic and common stronghold the enemy uses to ensnare and unknowingly impact everyone. Satan is the accuser of man, and this tactic is corrupting in the masses. People are most often ensnared by source-switching through ignorance or deception. So, what is it exactly? Source switching is choosing the counterfeit version of God and/or good and the counterfeit God and/or good is connected to a demonic source. It appears as something good, provides correct information, and helps and empowers people, but it is ultimately attached to something demonic at its root or core.

Let's take a flower for example. It is a scientific fact that the underground roots determine the overall health of the flower. So, no matter how beautiful the flower is above ground, if the roots of the plants are fed by a contaminated source (natural) or a demonic/evil source (spiritual), it ultimately becomes rooted from a contaminated or demonic source.

Another way to look at this is using the slavery times octoroon rule, now considered offensive. In slavery days, if a person had any portion of African American ancestry even as small as one-eighth, the person was considered to be Black or African American. Over time, in urban and slang vernacular, this was renamed to the "one drop" rule. If you had one drop of Black (African American) blood, they classified you as being from African American ancestry, therefore Black, even if you had the physical appearance of another race.

Applying the same principle to the demonic realm, if there is one drop of demonic activity or origin, it is demonic. No matter how good it looks, how much good it does, or how innocent it seems. If the source is rooted or plugged into something that stems from the demonic, it is demonic.

Does this make sense? Let's go back to the power source example. Imagine God has a power grid or power plant, and the devil has a power grid or power plant as well. As long as everything works correctly, it would be possible to obtain electrical power from either source. However, although you have electrical power does not mean you are pulling from the correct power source. As Believers, it is imperative, that we know the source. The roots matter. Believers need to know their source and ensure that everything they associate themselves with is connected to the correct "power" source.

The enemy/devil is a mocker and a deceiver. He wants you willingly or unwillingly. If it requires tricking you into connecting to his power source, he will trick you. He has no problem pretending to be an angel of light, as long as he has you rooted to him by switching the source of the power. Again, this can be done without your knowledge. You must check all your power sources. The root of a thing matters.

Examples of Source-Switching

The enemy constantly uses this tactic because it is so easy to pull off. The goal is for you to be distracted, just going along with the flow of things. The enemy is not trying to scare you because you will retreat. He wants you fully engaged and accepting. Source-switching hides out in the open. Things that seem good, feel harmless, informational, productive, and civic-minded all could be tools for source-switching. How, you ask? Typically, you do not question the roots of origin of something good, but you should. It could stem from the demonic realm.

The next few sections will probably upset the status quo. I understand what you are about to read will be disturbing and rejected by many, but so is Christ. It is important for me to get this information out in a non-judgmental, non-condemning way. In full disclosure and transparency, I have taken part in everything listed below. No one, but God himself, would have convinced me I was operating outside His will. I chose the "red pill" when I accepted Jesus as my personal Lord and Savior. My walk with God has always been critically important in my life. So, when God began to remove the scales from my eyes and He began revealing these missteps in my walk, I was stunned and, sometimes, heartbroken and sickened by the information I learned. *There is a way that seems right to a man, but its end is the way of death. Proverbs 14:12*

There's a scene in The Matrix movie, where Neo is in denial about the information, he learned about the deceptive world called the Matrix, and he was screaming "This isn't real" and Cypher says, "He's about to pop" and Neo vomited in front of everyone right where he stood. The weight of the reality presented to him was too much for him to handle. I had a similar reaction when I learned many things I was connected to or taken part in were connected to the wrong spiritual source, and source switching had happened to me.

Horoscopes, Astrology, & Zodiac Signs

I know this may be difficult to hear but horoscopes, astrology, and zodiac signs are all connected to the wrong source. It is possible to get accurate information by using these methods, but the source of the connection has demonic roots. Its source is from the demonic realm.

> *"When you come into the land that the Lord your God is giving you, you shall not learn to follow the abominable practices of those nations. There shall not be found among you anyone who burns his son or his daughter as an offering, anyone who practices divination or tells fortunes or interprets omens, or a sorcerer or a charmer or a medium or a necromancer or one who inquires of the dead." Deuteronomy 18:9-11*

"Astrology is the "interpretation" of an assumed influence the stars (and planets) exert on human destiny. According to astrology, the sign you were born under, Aquarius, Pisces, Aries, Taurus, Gemini, Cancer, Leo, Virgo, Libra, Scorpio, Sagittarius, or Capricorn, impacts your destiny. This is a false belief."[9] God is the controller and ruler of all destinies. Most people can tell you their astrological sign as quickly as they can recite their name. Your astrological sign is not your identity, and you empower the enemy and berate God each time you say the name of God (I AM) + your astrological sign name.

When a person states, "I am a zodiac sign". You have evoked the power of I AM. God's word cannot return void and you have pronounced a curse on yourself by accepting the spirit and characteristics of the zodiac sign. This has been around for centuries, and it is perfectly acceptable and normal for our culture and society, even in the church. "In His word, Deuteronomy 18:10, God clearly states that we should not use divination or sorcery but instead rely on Him to understand humanity better and His will."[10]

> "And when you look up into the sky and see the sun, moon, and stars — all the forces of heaven — do not be seduced into worshiping them. The Lord your God gave them to all the peoples of the earth." Deuteronomy 4:19

"You may wonder why God would not want you to think in your zodiac sign. In His Scripture, God has made it clear how he feels about us seeking guidance and clarity from any other source except the Bible. When we believe in Zodiac signs, we essentially believe in an astrologist's interpretation, not God's. We depend on the alignment of the stars and planets to affect and direct our personality or future."[11]

Paganism in Popular Holidays and Celebrations

Pagan practices have infiltrated many of our favorite holidays. Paganism is the authentic religion of ancient Greece and Rome, as well as the surrounding areas, in the strictest sense. Pagan comes from the Latin word *paganus*, which means "country dweller"; paganism can refer to polytheism or the worship of more than one god. A pagan is also considered to be one who, for the most part, has no religion and indulges in worldly delights and material possessions; someone who revels in sensual pleasures; a hedonistic or self-indulgent individual.[12]

The church has been infiltrated and perpetuates many pagan practices. Christmas and Easter are the two most recognized offenders. They seem normal and harmless. They are enjoyable. It's the happiest time of the year. In recent years, the church has attempted to acknowledge its weaknesses by emphasizing Jesus during Christmas and changing the name of Easter to Resurrection Sunday, but these efforts only address the issue on a surface-level.

I acknowledge this may be a gut punch for many. I remember the hurt and agony I went through, so I will only provide a few examples and encourage everyone to do their research. The point I want to concentrate on is about source-switching.

A recognizable example is a popular Christmas song that has lyrics referring to "make the yuletide gay". What is a yuletide? In ancient yuletides "Yule, or jól, was a midwinter festival celebrated by Germanic peoples, and it fell sometime in between mid-November and early January...During Yule, a sacrifice would be made, and the blood would be smeared on idols."[13]

"Yule is celebrated by Pagans and in most forms of Wicca as an alternative to Christmas. Often, the holiday is celebrated at winter solstice. In both religions, the holiday celebrates the rebirth of the sun. In 2013, over 3,500 people gathered for a Yuletide celebration at Stonehenge to watch the sunrise."[14] Santa Claus, Christmas trees, mistletoe, holly, and more are all source-switched things. My responsibility is only to relay the information. You may believe I'm being too literal, but do your research. I have fulfilled my obligation.

> *When he sees the sword coming upon the land, if he blows the trumpet and warns the people, then whoever hears the sound of the trumpet and does not take warning, if the sword comes and takes him away, his blood shall be on his own head. He heard the sound of the trumpet but did not take warning; his blood shall be upon himself. But he who takes warning will [a]save his life. But*

> *if the watchman sees the sword coming and does not blow the trumpet, and the people are not warned, and the sword comes and takes any person from among them, he is taken away in his iniquity; but his blood I will require at the watchman's hand.' Ezekiel 33:3-6*

Source-Switch Complications

Fear, pain, sickness, heartbreak, rejection, loneliness, and suffering are all things most people want to avoid. They are also the very things that will make you question and ask, "Where is God?" Why did He allow this to happen to me? The most famous and unanswered question to anyone's satisfaction is: Why does God allow bad things to happen to good people?

If we are not careful, these times of discomfort will open the door to the enemy and cause a source-switch. The devil doesn't care how he gets you, as long as he gets you. If he can use your rejection, depression, heartbreak, or pain to make you reject God and move to his outlet, He will. We are at the greatest risk when we are vulnerable.

Jesus experienced every affliction. He knows and understands what we go through from his own experiences. The devil came to Jesus hoping to tempt him. Testing to see if Jesus could be tempted. So, if the Son of God is challenged with temptation what makes you believe that you cannot be tempted or would not endure a similar trial? So, during periods of trials and hardships, when I want to question God, instead I ask this question: when did we read about or hear about Jesus experiencing a similar trial? For those who jumped to counter with romantic relationship problems, the Bible is filled with dramatic relationship issues for you to choose and learn from.

We must resist the urge to look outside of God for answers. I had a friend who was a minister. My Minister friend was going through a difficult season and had been praying, but the trials kept coming. During this time, a mutual friend of ours told her about this awesome session she had with a medium. This was a friend whom she cared about and trusted. She mentioned how the medium provided answers to questions and how accurate and spot-on she was with the information she provided. This information came at just the right time, at a moment of weakness, and my minster friend agreed to have a session. I was not informed about it before it happened. Do not judge. If life hits you in the right way, you too may succumb and have a weak moment.

My minister friend told me about the session as soon as it was over. Both the minister and the mutual friend felt in their spirits that something was not right. My Minister friend spiraled into self-condemnation and further despair. The devil had tricked them and now they felt unworthy. If I'm being truthful, I was shocked, but I understood what happened. It was a source-switch.

An easy example to consider is brand name items versus high-quality knock-offs. Ladies may understand this better. For the longest time, I wanted a designer purse, however, I could not afford one. While shopping at the flea market, I came across a NY Canal Street vendor who had what looked to be designer bags. Only after a super close inspection could you identify the bag as a fake or knock-off. Sometimes the fake looked so real it was impossible to tell.

This is the peril of source-switching. The enemy will present you with exactly what God can give you, but it's plugged into the wrong spiritual source. So, in the case of my minister friend, they received accurate information from the medium, spot on in fact, but the information was derived by a demonic method and source. The medium used divination to obtain accurate information. The enemy had lured my minister friend and mutual friend and sullied them both into a dangerous space where they both could stand accused.

We discussed it and everyone agreed that repentance was the course of action needed to correct this misstep. We also agreed they needed to cast away any self-condemnation because we all fall short of the glory of God, and rarely do we fall in the way we would expect to fall. If gambling is your temptation or weak point, you will be on guard for that, so the enemy will go to the unguarded areas of your life to infiltrate. So, it is imperative to consider the source in all things.

Spiritual Vertigo

Except for childbirth, vertigo was the most unsettling medical condition I have ever experienced. "Vertigo is a sensation that the surrounding environment is spinning in circles. It can make you feel dizzy and off-balance."[15] Besides headaches, I didn't experience any pain with vertigo. What I experienced was dizziness, constant swaying, and a constant feeling of unbalance, almost to the point of falling. At times, I felt like I was trapped on a fast-moving and winding rollercoaster. It was a disconcerting experience.

I reference the experience because I experienced a similar phenomenon with God when he began uncovering truths that were causing missteps in my walk with him. These revelations caught me off guard. I couldn't seem to find my balance or sturdy ground. Up to this point in my salvation walk, I felt I was doing everything to the best of my ability to walk with Christ.

One of my continuous prayers is not to be on the wrong side of right. Meaning, I don't want to think I'm doing something correctly, only to have it be wrong in the sight of the Lord. Well, God in his infinite grace and mercy decided to answer that prayer, and the revelation sent me into a state of spiritual vertigo.

The revelation was regarding an organization I belonged to and the source-switching that was being ignored. Now just to show you how we treat God sometimes, after praying and requesting that God show me any missteps, when He did, I did not want to believe the revelation. I kept going back and forth, Christians founded the organization. That didn't matter. The organization was home to preachers, politicians, entertainers, and extremely prominent people. That didn't matter. The organization provided me with lifelong friendships. That didn't matter. I have family in the same organization, that didn't matter. The organization did a myriad of good across the globe and financially helped, supported, and undergirded people in communities across the world. That didn't matter. The organization had and continues to have a reputation for great work. That didn't matter.

What mattered to God, and what He revealed to me, was regarding the foundational source of the organization and the source roots of the initiation process. That was the issue. Both stemmed from freemasonry, which has ties to demonic beliefs and roots, and because of that, my membership with my organization was an unholy covenant to the demonic realm. That was it. So, I literally tried to negotiate and explain to God that the people (the founders of the organization) cannot be held responsible for what they don't know... which God met me with, but I just told you, so now you know.

As much as I hated to admit it, my eyes had been opened. I could not deny the truth, and I would be forced to make a change I never expected to make. Now let me be clear, this wasn't an instant change of course for me. I went back and forth, praying, asking for clarity, and confirmation after confirmation. It was a three-year tug-of-war for me to be certain and to make the final decision.

Ironically, I thought deciding to leave the organization was the end, but it was actually the beginning of a rabbit hole full of revelation God wanted to impart to me. However, before He could give me these revelations, I had to be purged from the attachments to the demonic realm and renounce and denounce my affiliations before I could move forward with God and the work, He wanted me to do for Him.

Leaving my organization required a process called renouncement. I had to renounce the organization and upon further spiritual research, I found out I had to denounce as well. "Renounce means to give up or relinquish or declare your ending support".[16] "Denounce means to condemn openly, accuse publicly, or formally end a treaty."[17] The renouncement process intensified the spiritual vertigo. I was literally in a state of disbelief and felt scared, unsettled, and confused. I was worried about my friendships inside the organization, and what people in similar organizations would think. It was a tremendous ordeal. What confused me the most about renouncing my membership was I had not been active in the organization at all. Soon after I joined, I got married, had children, and ran into health issues. So, I was a member on paper after undergraduate graduation. I refused to wear the organization's paraphernalia because I didn't want to be known as a "letter wearer".

Truthfully, no one in my adult life knew I was in the organization unless I told them. There was nothing in my life that represented the organization, so why did I have such a visceral reaction about leaving? I hadn't made any contributions since I graduated, so no one would notice my absence. It was a spiritual hold. I subsequently discovered it wasn't me resisting to leave, it was the demonic stronghold encouraging me to resist God and remain in the organization.

The covenants I had made with unknown entities when I took part in the initiation were rebelling against me leaving. I depended completely on God for everything outside of what I could see to sustain me as I went through the process of renouncement and denouncement, and it was a process. It sent me into a spiritual spiral, spiritual vertigo. However, thank God for Jesus. He never left me nor abandoned me. He was with me every step of the way. I think it is critically important for me to outline what I experienced.

It was difficult for me to come to terms with the fact I had aligned myself with something that put my soul at risk of damnation for something I didn't even know about or understand. There are so many Bible verses I grew up with, warning against this exact thing. These Bible verses were repeated so much, that they were almost cliché. It wasn't until I was going through that the meaning and application of the verses opened up for me. This is why the Bible emphatically warns you to study to show yourself approved and that there is a way that seems right to a man that leads to destruction.

> *There is a way that seems right to a man, but its end is the way of death. Proverbs 14:12*
>
> *Be diligent to present yourself approved to God, a worker who does not need to be ashamed, rightly dividing the word of truth. 2 Timothy 2:15*
>
> *And I set my heart to seek and search out by wisdom concerning all that is done under heaven; this burdensome task God has given to the sons of man, by which they may be exercised Ecclesiastes 1:13*

This process of renouncement/denouncement taught me so many things about spiritual warfare, demonic realms, spiritual wickedness in high places, and the power required to battle on this level. Now you may ask what level? When you decide to renounce/denounce secret organizations, a process is required. Similar to a marriage, if you walk away from your marriage and spouse, but you never file for a divorce, you are still married. To end your marriage covenant you must file for divorce. To end your covenant ties to your organization, you must renounce/denounce. You must sever the covenant ties.

In this circumstance, renouncement for me was turning away from the organization in the natural by filing paperwork with the National Headquarters of the organization. They will instruct you on the process. Spiritually, denouncement was required by pronouncing my actions as evil and repenting to God through a sincere prayer of my association with it. For clarification, what I pronounced as evil was the foundational origins of the Freemason ties.

I came across denouncement and renouncement prayers online, read them soberly, and decided that they would be useful in my process. I added to the prayers to make it authentic to me and speak my heart to God and repent. What I wasn't prepared for was how many demonic entities I would repent for aligning myself with entities unbeknownst to me.

Just so we are clear, let's take a step back for a minute and slow this down so you can understand what I am saying. When I was a child, I loved mythology, Greek or Roman, it didn't matter. My teachers introduced me to Greek and Roman mythology in school. The stories of these people intrigued me and kept my interest. As part of my studies, I was required to know the names of Greek and Roman mythology characters. For example, the Roman goddess Venus is the Greek goddess Aphrodite. Our teacher made us learn about the differences in the stories between the two versions as part of our studies and tested our knowledge.

I don't believe they teach mythology in school anymore, and, knowing what I know now, I'm not sure why they taught it then. I believe it was foreshadowing for today. I could never imagine how relevant and important those mythology lessons would be in my life.

Fast forward to today, while reading the renouncement/denouncement prayers, I encountered the same names of the gods and goddesses I learned about that needed to be renounced/denounced depending on the organization. Imagine my dismay.

The spiritual warfare I encountered trying to separate myself from my organization was immense. Now remember I told you I had not actively taken part in any activities for almost twenty-five years, if not longer. However, the minute I was resolute about severing the relationship, I was fighting on a spiritual level I had never experienced. Why you ask? Those Greek and Roman mythology gods and goddesses were nephilim, men of renown as described in the Bible and the Book of Enoch which we discussed earlier.

> *There were giants on the earth in those days, and also afterward, when the sons of God came into the daughters of men and they bore children to them. Those were the mighty men who were of old, men of renown. Genesis 6: 4-5*

I had to come to terms with the fact that I was renouncing and denouncing a nephilim spirit affiliation that I unknowingly attached myself to when taking ritual oaths to join my organization. Again, just to reiterate, nephilim are the children of women and fallen angels.

Reconciling my natural mind to spiritual warfare was a process. The enemy will try to convince you that you are losing your mind. When you go through the initiation process, you are making a covenant relationship with the women who go through the process with you. They are called your line sisters or line brothers.

So, if your line sister carries any type of generational curse like chronic illness, autoimmune disorders, infertility, poverty, adultery, all the women never marry, divorce, fractured marriages, drugs, and alcohol abuse, promiscuity, or gluttony, guess what you might find yourself fighting one day too? All because of this covenant bond made on an unholy foundation. Try to wrap your mind around that for a minute. Wrestling with this information, I found myself at the feet of Jesus. I sounded crazy to myself, but I bet Noah felt crazy too when God told him to build an ark for a flood when rain was an unfamiliar concept to him and his community. Selah.

> *By faith Noah, being divinely warned of things not yet seen, moved with godly fear, prepared an ark for the saving of his household, by which he condemned the world and became heir of the righteousness which is according to faith.*
> Hebrews 11:7

For people who belong to BGLO organizations, there is a brief section at the end of the book that goes into a little more detail. I'm not here to pass judgment, just information, revealed to me by God. Do with it what you want, but you can never deny you were not told or didn't know after this point. The mere fact that you are reading this book is a sign that God is trying to reveal something to you. Please do not turn away.

The Essence of Time

Time is a debated topic. It is familiar to everyone, yet difficult to explain. Theologians, Scientists, and philosophers will all provide a different definition, but most agree on how to measure it. "Physicists define time as the progression of events from the past to the present into the future. Basically, if a system is unchanging, it is timeless. Physicists consider time as the fourth dimension of reality, which they use to describe events in three-dimensional space."[18] This is the mainstream and widely accepted definition of time. It is not something we can see, touch, or taste, but we can measure its passage."[19] Our current structures to measure time are the calendar and the clock. I don't know about you, but I have battled with both the calendar and the clock over the years. Don't get me wrong, I am completely grateful for the time I have, but that clock and calendar have had me in a tailspin at certain times in my life.

Time creates urgency. Urgency is a feeling of importance or immediacy that arises when one feels the need to act quickly or decisively in response to a crucial cause. It can be triggered by a variety of factors including deadlines, emergencies, or unexpected events."[20]

Because of all the competing thoughts on time, the Believer must know where God is in relation to time. As we already discussed in the definition of time, Man/people live in the four-dimensional physical realm. John 4:24 states that God is a spirit. God does not exist within our physical time. God dwells in the spiritual realm and the confines of our physical laws and the dimensions that govern our world do not limit him.[21] God created time, but the rules of time do not apply to him. Why should the Creator submit to the creation?

God transcends time, so His perspective on time would differ vastly from ours. The Bible tells us a thousand years in our time is like a day in God's sight (Psalm 90:4). So why does any of this matter?

The urgent nature of this book is about us/man/people, not God. God, who lives outside of time, already knows how all of this will end before anyone enters eternity with Him. This book is, in part, about the choices you will make for your eternal soul. God exists in the realm he does now, without man. He will continue to do so with or without man. He sent his Son Jesus Yeshua the Christ to die for us so we will be able to reach him one day and spend eternity with him. However, we have a foe, an adversary that will do anything to keep us from reaching that ultimate goal. Think of this as a warning, just like the warning Noah gave to his people. He told them rain was coming, a massive amount of rain. Noah delivered this message to a people who had never seen or experienced rain.

The Days of Noah Are Now

> *"And as it was in the days of Noah, so it will be also in the days of the Son of Man: They ate, they drank, they married wives, they were given in marriage, until the day that Noah entered the ark, and the flood came and destroyed them all. Likewise, as it was also in the days of Lot: They ate, they drank, they bought, they sold, they planted, they built; but on the day that Lot went out of Sodom it rained fire and brimstone from heaven and destroyed them all. Even so will it be in the day when the Son of Man is revealed." (Luke 17:26-30)*

In this passage, Jesus is speaking about the coming Kingdom of God. Jesus tells us the end times will be like the days of Noah. What were the days of Noah like? Idolatry characterized the days of Noah with multiple gods, debauchery, sexual immorality, blood rituals, corruption, lawlessness, and God-less leadership. When comparing today with those days, we cannot overlook the similarity.

God has focused my concentration for the last two decades on the spiritual world, so that is where I will make my comparisons. However, I came across a comprehensive list from Rick Renner that outlined the characteristics of the days of Noah.[22]

Bible	Characteristic
Genesis 6:1	**—A Time of an Exploding Population** Today there is a population boom like never before — just as it occurred in the days before the Flood.
Genesis 6:2	**— A Time of Sexual Perversion** Today there is widespread sexual perversion on a scale beyond anything we have known — very much like what occurred in the days before the Flood.
Genesis 6:2	**— A Time of Dark Spiritual Activity** Today there is enormously dark spiritual activity occurring, especially in Western civilization — very similar to what occurred in the days before the Flood.
Genesis 6:4	**— A Time When Transhumanism Occurred** Today scientists are tampering with "gender and genetics," and it's creating monstrous things — very much like what happened when monsters appeared in the world before the Flood.
Genesis 6:5	**— A Time When Evil Was Continually in the Heart of Man** Today we are seeing inventions of evil unlike anything our generation has ever witnessed — and it is absolutely similar to what was happening in the days before the Flood.
Genesis 6:11	**— A Time of Widespread Violence** Today we are seeing anarchy, rebellion, and violence spreading its tentacles across the earth — a replication of events that occurred in the earth in the days before the Flood.

Reprinted from As It Was in the Days of Noah | Renner Ministries [22]

The wickedness and depravity of mankind made God regret his decision to make man. Before the flood man's life span lasted hundreds of years. God reduced man's lifespan to one hundred and twenty years after the flood.

> *And the Lord said, "My Spirit shall not strive with man forever, for he is indeed flesh; yet his days shall be one hundred and twenty years." There were giants on the earth in those days, and also afterward, when the sons of God came into the daughters of men and they bore children to them. Those were the mighty men who were of old, men of renown. Then the Lord saw that the wickedness of man was great in the earth, and that every intent of the thoughts of his heart was only evil continually. And the Lord was sorry that He had made man on the earth, and He was grieved in His heart. So the Lord said, "I will destroy man whom I have created from the face of the earth, both man and beast, creeping thing and birds of the air, for I am sorry that I have made them." But Noah found grace in the eyes of the Lord. (Genesis 6: 3-8).*

In the Days of Noah, it was not unusual to ask, "What God do you serve?" or "What God do you worship?" Currently, within America Christianity is still the most popular religion with approximately 70.6% of the population identifying as Christian, however, there still are 22.8% of Americans identified as unaffiliated or unassociated with any religion. That is four times more than Judaism (1.9%), Islam (0.9%), Buddhism (0.7%), Hinduism (0.7%), and other religions (0.3%) combined.[23]

There is a falling away from God and a non-belief in God like we have never seen before. Over the last five years, especially since Covid, there has been a significant growth in the number of people who claim spirituality, but not God per se. The number of new age, satanic/luciferian, pagan, druidry practices that have infiltrated the church is startling, but God is raising up his people called to this time to help people understand their souls are at risk.

God, in his benevolence, provided Noah with a hundred years to build the ark and provide an opportunity for people to turn from their depravity and wickedness. Noah was successful in building the ark, but not the latter. I don't know if God will grant another hundred years for man to spread the message and help people understand, but you cannot deny that our times resemble those of Noah, and the signs show that humanity's time is running out.

Now, from a spiritual vantage point, I think it is important to not just compare the day-to-day living of the Days of Noah, but the spiritual climate of the times. As I stated before, it was not unusual to ask "What God do you serve?" People worshipped many types of gods, deities, and idols. Mainstream American Christians have become complacent and arrogant enough to believe that when a person says they believe in God, they believe in the one true God (YHWH, The God of Abraham, Isaac, and Israel (Jacob). The enemy has upped the ante in his vile disrespect and blasphemy towards God. He is constantly trying to insert and apply the title "creator" to his kind, and he continues to use man as the pawn in his plan. In the Days of Noah, there were mass abominations taking place. The Book of Enoch, an Ethiopian Cannon, and a controversial book of the Apocrypha describes the debauchery that was taking place. It is important to note the Apocrypha is not the Bible, and it is considered non-canonical and non-inspired, by Theologians. For my babes in Christ, my new Christians and converts the Apocrypha is not equivalent to the Bible. They are not on equal footing*.

Excerpts From the Book of Enoch:

[Enoch 6:1] And it came to pass, when the sons of men had increased, that in those days there were born to them fair and beautiful daughters. [Enoch 6:2] And the Angels, the sons of Heaven, saw them and desired them. And they said to one another: "Come, let us choose for ourselves wives, from the children of men, and let us beget, for ourselves, children." [Enoch 6:3] And Semyaza, who was their leader, said to them: "I fear that you may not wish this deed to be done and that I alone will pay for this great sin." [Enoch 6:4] And they all answered him, and said: "Let us all swear an oath, and bind one-another with curses, so not to alter this plan, but to carry out this plan effectively." [Enoch 6:5] Then they all swore together and all bound one another with curses to it. [Enoch 6:6] And they were, in all, two hundred and they came down on Ardis, which is the summit of Mount Hermon. And they called the mountain Hermon because on it they swore and bound one another with curses [Enoch 6:7] And these are the names of their leaders: Semyaza, who was their leader, Urakiba, Ramiel, Kokabiel, Tamiel, Ramiel, Daniel, Ezeqiel, Baraqiel, Asael, Armaros, Batriel, Ananel,

Zaqiel, Samsiel, Satael, Turiel, Yomiel, Araziel. [Enoch 6:8] These are the leaders of the two hundred Angels and of all the others with them. [Enoch 7:1] And they took wives for themselves and everyone chose for himself one each. And they began to go into them and were promiscuous with them. And they taught them charms and spells, and they showed them the cutting of roots and trees. [Enoch 7:2] And they became pregnant and bore large giants. And their height was three thousand cubits. [Enoch 7:3] These devoured all the toil of men; until men were unable to sustain them. [Enoch 7:4] And the giants turned against them in order to devour men. [Enoch 7:5] And they began to sin against birds, and against animals, and against reptiles, and against fish, and they devoured one another's flesh, and drank the blood from it. [Enoch 7:6] Then the Earth complained about the lawless ones. [Enoch 8:1] And Azazel taught men to make swords, and daggers, and shields, and breastplates. And he showed them the things after these, and the art of making them; bracelets, and ornaments, and the art of making up the eyes, and of beautifying the eyelids, and the most precious stones, and all kinds of coloured dyes. And the world was changed. [Enoch 8:2] And there was great impiety, and much fornication, and they went astray, and all their ways became corrupt. [Enoch 8:3] Amezarak taught all those who cast spells and cut roots, Armaros the release of spells, and Baraqiel astrologers, and Kokabiel portents, and Tamiel taught astrology, and Asradel taught the path of the Moon. [Enoch 8:4] And at the destruction of men they cried out; and their voices reached Heaven.[24]

From this passage in Enoch which mimics Genesis 6, but goes into much more detail, we see the Nephilim* teaching man wickedness. The wickedness that is mentioned are things people in current times know about, practice, or fully incorporate into their conversations and everyday lives without a second thought. Abortion, Root working, witchcraft and the casting of spells, burning sage, tarot cards, Ouija boards, crystals, and astrology are not of God. Many of these things have been source-switched. However how many can we honestly say we are not familiar with these things, even if we do not participate in them?

During the days of Noah, nephilim introduced abortion, necromancy, sorcery, astrology, DNA manipulation, and many other atrocities. They used their supernatural knowledge and made many sacrileges and abominations. You cannot take God's perfected creations, animals, and man, and think you can improve upon them. The unmitigated gall. The transfer of knowledge to man made the nephilim appear like gods because of their supernatural abilities. Man began to worship these abominations, called them gods, and incorporated their depraved and sick rituals into their lives. Human sacrifice, blood drinking, burning babies, and other atrocities all stem from Fallen angels (demons) and the children they had with humans (nephilim).

The devil/enemy and all his unholy hierarchical affiliates used supernatural abilities to deceive Man. They are still using supernatural tactics to trick man. From this, we learn a timeless lesson, that all supernatural activity is not of God. Every voice you hear is not God. God tells you to test the spirits:

> *Beloved, do not believe every spirit, but test the spirits, whether they are of God; because many false prophets have gone out into the world. By this you know the Spirit of God: Every spirit that confesses that Jesus Christ has come in the flesh is of God, and every spirit that does not confess that Jesus Christ has come in the flesh is not of God. And this is the spirit of the Antichrist, which you have heard was coming, and is now already in the world. (1 John 4:1-6)*

Today, we are dealing with the introduction of transhumanism. This is not science; this is man infringing on creation reaching back to the Days of Noah. The introduction of Artificial intelligence (AI), while seemingly harmless right now and offering many conveniences with time savings, I urge you to resist it. You are being baited and groomed for what it will grow up to become. Believe me, I understand the lure of it, I battle it every day. This book could have been written in three days with the assistance of AI technology, but knowing the source of its origins, I resisted.

I'm not going to lie, it is a battle for me, but I keep asking myself if convenience and time-savings is worth my soul. I keep going back to God because I'm sure there was someone in Thomas Edison's and Tesla's time who thought the light bulb or electricity was evil. Just do your research and pray.

Now let me say this I'm providing the information; each person has to work it out for themselves with God. Just know, every person will have to stand alone before God to answer for how we lived our life. Just know in the end the devil will turn around and accuse man for participating in the very debauchery, he initiated. Being covered in the blood of Jesus matters. No one comes to the Father, except through Jesus.

Urgent War Cry
Part II

The Essence of Time

Time is short. We are living in the Days of Noah right now. Times have shifted to the advantage of the enemy. Systems of the demonic realm are in place. Witchcraft and sorcery practitioners have placed a spirit of darkness over the world through rituals, blood sacrifices, and other enchantments. Because we live in a social media age, if we do not see it, we don't believe it. But the Body of Christ follows different rules. We walk by faith and not by sight. Just like he did for Peter after he betrayed him, Jesus is coming to us, right where we are. Here is the good news: Jesus is healing the blindness of his people! The spirit of darkness will lift. 2024 is starting off to be a year of exposure, revelation, and judgment. Even the secular world is crying out "The truth don't need any motivation…There is only God's way or the other way" ~Katt Williams.[25]

Jesus is the Truth, The Light, and the Way. No one shall come to the Father except through Jesus. This is an urgent war cry. There is a spiritual shaking going on and God is changing the guard. Those in obscurity with gifts and callings, your time is now. Rise, stand up, and heed the call of your Savior. There is more work to be done and wars to fight, but I warn you, your lifestyle must match your walk and your mouth. We are in the age of the false prophets. The bible warned us. Nevertheless, we are called to be a light in dark places, but be careful with where and who you assemble with during these times.

This is the enemy's time, and he will continue to tear you down and tempt you with elevated and targeted deceptions, perversions, and defilement of your gifts. The enemy is coming after you with custom-made deception. He is not coming at you with things he knows you are gifted to see. He is attacking the blind spots. You need to shore up your blind spots and cover yourself and your family.

In the case of intercessors and those involved in the Deliverance Ministry, it is necessary to address your blind spots, pray against demonic mantles and altars, and surround the principality regions with prayer. This is a turbulent time for those called to this work. Possession has shifted. People are allowing themselves to be inhabited by spirits. People are engaging and playing with the occult because it is being presented as acceptable or under the guise of religious belief. Television and the Media celebrate evil. There is a show called Lucifer and a television show called Evil. Both were network hits with social media fan bases.

For this work, you must consecrate and anoint yourself. You cannot be chasing "likes" or monetization on social media. If that is a byproduct of your ministry, so be it, but if that is the only reason you are in it, get out. If you are not called to this work, leave it alone. Just focus on covering and praying for those who have been appointed to that ministry. This is an urgent call to self-correct. Get the speck out of your eye. God loves you and he doesn't want to lose one soul.

For Unbelievers, God loves you. Jesus, his Son died for your sins. You can see the craziness in the world, and you're scared. You are looking to fill that void. Jesus can answer all those questions hidden deep in your heart. He wants to form a relationship with you. You can't possibly imagine you are reading this book and got to this point by accident. There are no coincidences. There has been a tugging at your heart. You are searching for answers. Jesus, Yeshua the Christ, is the answer. Please recite the simple prayer at the end of this section and begin your relationship with Jesus today. You will not regret it.

To those experiencing supernatural events and/or feeling scared and tortured every day. You could be experiencing heavy attacks from the demonic realm. Examples are having night terrors, experiencing sleep paralysis, and hearing constant voices instructing you to hurt yourselves or others. You feel like someone is watching you. The things you are experiencing are too bizarre, you dare not tell anyone. There is an explanation for all of it but the most important thing to know right now is <u>God is a deliverer</u>. He can free you from that torture. You are an open vessel that needs to be shored up with the protection of the Holy Spirit. Invite Jesus into your heart. If you are in therapy for any of the aforementioned things, please do not discontinue your therapy, just add Jesus to your therapeutic plan. Jesus makes everything better.

For those of you with lifelong covenant ties to organizations, I beg you to investigate what I have said, look into what is being told to you, and take it all back to God. Ask God if you have unknowingly formed a connection with demonic entities. Ask Him to reveal if you have co-mingled and came away with something unknown to you. Ask God to reveal anything to you that may be keeping you from Him? I know you love your organization and your affiliations. I did too, but is it worth your soul, Brother, Sister? Is it worth your soul? **Please read the special section at the end of this book.**

For Believers examine your life, your covenant ties, your self-erected idols. What gets more of your attention than God? It's time for God to go back to the top of the list. Cast down your idols. I'm here to let you know it is possible to be affiliated with demonic ties without knowing it. Pray that God removes all scales from your eyes. There is an attack of blindness that is associated with this attack. Cast blindness down, in the name of Jesus. Pray for revelation about hidden things. Pray Jeremiah 33:3 over your life but hold on when you do because God will reveal things to you. His word will not return void.

"This is the time of fulfillment. The kingdom of God is at hand. Repent, and believe the Gospel" Mark 1:15. God is coming back. If you are reading this work, it is not by coincidence. God is crying out to you and the remnant in Christ. You are an end-time warrior. Stand up and take your proper place. Rise up because there are giants to stand against in the spiritual realm, but you must clean your armor from demonic attachments or alliances. Talk to God and do what he tells you to do. Amen.

A Call to Repentance

"Now, therefore," says the Lord, "Turn to Me with all your heart, with fasting, with weeping, and with mourning." So rend your heart, and not your garments; Return to the Lord your God, For He is gracious and merciful, Slow to anger, and of great kindness; And He relents from doing harm. Who knows if He will turn and relent, And leave a blessing behind Him—A grain offering and a drink offering For the Lord your God? Joel 2:12-13

Prayer of Repentance:

Father God, I come to you in prayer asking for the forgiveness of my sins. I want to repent for all my sins known and unknown and I invite you into my life. I confess with my mouth and believe in my heart that Jesus is your Son, and that he died on the cross at Calvary for my forgiveness and eternal life in the Kingdom of Heaven. Father God, I believe Jesus rose from the dead, and I ask you right now to come into my life and be my personal Lord and Savior. I want an everlasting relationship with you. Because your word is truth, I confess with my mouth that I am saved, born again and cleansed by the Blood of Jesus! Thank you for Salvation. In Jesus name, Amen.

Well, my assignment is done. Here now is my final conclusion:

> *Fear God and obey his commands, for this is everyone's duty. God will judge us for everything we do, including every secret thing, whether good or bad. Ecclesiastes 12:13-14*

Special Section FOR BGLO & Secret Societies

Secret Societies and Black Greek Lettered Organizations (BGLO)- For all my readers in BGLO please keep an open mind to this information and take it back to God. I am not attacking or judging you. I am not attacking your organizations or the work that they do. I have been where you are. You don't have to agree with a thing I say. Just ask God about what I am telling you. Engage him in this conversation. This was a three-year conversation for me with God, and it was difficult. I was a member of a BGLO and would have never chosen to leave my organization if it were not for God himself leading me on a journey of discovery and revelation.

This is the point: The origin story for all BGLO organizations was constructed on and modeled after freemasonry principles, formations, templates, and ideologies. Freemasonry at the highest levels reveals allegiance to the demonic.

Even if you take the position that it is a different organization, and you did not and do not believe in what they do, the affiliation at the creation of each group cannot be ignored. For my Believers/ Christians, we see a similar situation in the Bible when Paul was trying to mitigate the issue with the Corinthians if meat sacrificed to idols could be eaten by Christians. Here is what was said:

> *No, but the sacrifices of pagans are offered to demons, not to God, and I do not want you to be participants with demons. You cannot drink the cup of the Lord and the cup of demons too; you cannot have a part in both the Lord's table and the table of demons. Are we trying to arouse the Lord's jealousy? Are we stronger than he? 1 Corinthians 10: 20-22.*

I would urge you to read the entire tenth chapter of Corinthians, but I ask are we stronger than God brothers and sisters of BGLO's? At the core, secret societies and BGLOs have modeled their roots on masonic practices, ideologies, and templates. Masonic practices are demonic. One drop demonic IS demonic. The problem lies in the initiation process and ceremony; the oaths taken to get into the organization, and the deities attached to the organizations. Once your ceremony is over, congratulations, you have entered into a covenant with the demonic realm. The devil's purpose is to kill, steal, and destroy. It is so important for you to understand it is possible to align yourself unknowingly to the demonic realm. Believers are not exempt. This can happen to Believers.

The Bible tells us that there is a way that seems right to man that leads to hell. Even when you think you're doing the right thing, the devil has crafted this well-organized deception to attach demonic entities and generational curses on educated, civic, and mission-minded people. The devil doesn't care how he takes you down, as long as he takes you down. His mission is to keep you from the place he can't obtain, which is heaven.

I know each person can think of at least one person who drastically changed after they "went over". That change wasn't solely based on being hyped about the letters or that the organization gave them a boost of confidence. Unknowingly we have all witnessed the spiritual manifestation of a demon and it was shown in the physical realm. All the while friends and family are all claiming the person changed and not for the better. Everyone's demons manifest differently. Anyone in a BGLO knows exactly what I'm talking about, but it is not what you think it is. I'll stop there.

Please examine your shields carefully, pull out your initiation books, and re-read over the ceremonies you took part in and are now initiating people into then ask yourself these (5) five troublesome questions:

1) What oaths did you take?

But I say to you, do not take an oath at all, either by heaven, for it is the throne of God, or by the earth, for it is his footstool, or by Jerusalem, for it is the city of the great King. And do not take an oath by your head, for you cannot make one hair white or black. Let what you say be simply 'Yes' or 'No'; anything more than this comes from evil. Matthew 5:34-37

2) What Greek god or goddess is mentioned in your initiation ceremony or attached to your organization? In case you do not know please see below (please do not take my word for it research).

Who Are These False gods?

There is only ONE GOD—It is He who is the Alpha and Omega. Unfortunately, these groups mention, promote, and are connected to **Polytheism** (belief in multiple gods) and **Syncretism** (blending of beliefs) which are **against the Gospel of Jesus Christ**.

Following after false gods negatively affects our relationship with God. Do not be deceived by the amount of pastors, deacons, bishops, and gospel musicians who are in these organizations. People can think they are in good standing with God while skipping down the wide road to destruction.

The following false gods are attached to each organization (some are shown on their crests, others are mentioned in their rituals, while others have an indirect connection):

Sphinx: Egyptian mythical creature
Horus: Egyptian sun god

Qetesh: Semitic goddess (Syria) or Sumerian goddess of beauty, love & lust
Atlas: (shown on crest) Greek goddess
Themis: Titan goddess (mentioned in rituals)

Apollo: Greek god (in rituals)
Thoth: Egyptian god

Shekinah (aka Asherah/Ashtoreth/ Astarte) female goddess spirit in Kabbalah & Merkavah mysticism and Gnosticism (omega rituals refer to the spirit of omega who is female in nature)
Anubis: Egyptian god (depicted with a head of a jackal, which is a dog)

Minerva: Roman goddess of wisdom (shown on crest and in rituals)

What Does Scripture Say About Oaths?

In **Matthew 5:33-34** Jesus says, "Again you have heard that it was said...'You shall not swear falsely'...But I say to you, *do not swear at all*..."

Scripture is very clear that we should not make oaths AT ALL, however, the oaths taken when you crossed the burning sands are in opposition to the instruction given to us by Jesus Christ.

I urge you to think back to the oath you took and the words you said. Now compare those words and promises to what is written in the Bible.

As a Christian who can be honest with yourself, you will be uncomfortable with <u>many</u> of the words you repeated while joining your organization.

"I serve God through my organization"

Let's be honest, most service is not done to glorify Christ in sincere worship and honor, it's done in name of the fraternity/sorority.

When you are out in your sorority or fraternity paraphernalia and serving the community, what name is being promoted? Is it *really* the name of God?

Genesis 11:4 tells us of how the Tower of Babel was built. The people said, "...Let us make a name for ourselves..." God was so angry and displeased with the people, because at the core of their hearts was pride.

Many people genuinely believe these organizations are godly because they do community service, but this is not proof that they are godly. Furthermore, you cannot serve God/Yahweh in something He's not part of.

I will ask you this question: What stops you from gathering your friends and family together in order to serve others like you do with your organization?

Who Are These False gods continued...

Archon: Demon or underworld ruler in Gnosticism
Bastet: Egyptian cat-headed goddess

Horus: Egyptian god
Pallas Athena: Greek goddess of wisdom

Aurora: Roman goddess
Maat: Egyptian goddess

Centaur: Egyptian mythical creature

"I've never bowed down or worshipped another god in my organization."

Worship is not just about physically bowing to another god. *Worship* is defined as "the feeling or expression of reverence and adoration for a deity".

When you sing your organization's songs and sing to your organization, this is <u>a form of worship</u>. The worship songs are being sung to the spirit behind your organization.

In the very first Commandment, God says, "You shall have no other gods *before* me." (**Exodus 20:3**) over time people have taken this to mean do not believe in, follow, and worship another god.

In Hebrew Lexicon, "before" or עַל ('al-) means above; over; in addition to; together with. You cannot have another god *in addition* to the one, true God.

As a Christian, nothing should be on the same level in your life as God: this includes your family (**Matthew 10:37**), your job (**Matthew 4:18-22**), and your Greek-lettered organization.

Reprinted from Outfromamongthem.com Pamphlet: The Danger of Oaths: Who Did You Swear to Serve [26]

3) Do any of these organizations discriminate based on religion?

No, they do not. So, your line sister/ line brother can be a Satanist, luciferin, atheist, wiccan, or practice any non-Christian religion and you are binding yourself to that person in brotherhood or sisterhood and collectively taking an oath together on your knees. These are unholy covenants. God is intentional about covenants. What impact does this alignment have on your soul? Which spirits have you recently formed an unconscious connection with? What curses or generational curses are you adopting by aligning yourself and entering a lifelong covenant with your line sisters or line brothers? This is co-mingling at its core.

4) In whose name are you pledging devotion to, promising to serve?

Typically, you are pledging loyalty to the organization's name; you are chanting and singing in the organization's name.

> **Idolatry:** <u>extreme admiration, love, or reverence for something or someone.</u>

This is idolatry.

> *"'You shall have no other gods before me. Deuteronomy 5:7, Exodus 20:3*

5) Examine your hand symbols. What is the meaning of your hand symbols? What does the hand symbolize? Where are the symbols/animals/shapes (unofficial or official) used to represent your organization derived from? What other organizations use the same hand symbols and what does it mean there?

Symbolism is big. Research the hand symbols you flash. Look up outside of your organization and examine the animals and gods and goddesses associated with what you are doing.

> *Pay close attention to everything I have said to you. You must not invoke the names of other gods; they must not be heard on your lips. Exodus 23:13*
>
> *Be careful not to make a treaty with the inhabitants of the land you are entering, lest they become a snare in your midst. Exodus 34:12*

God does not play when it comes to covenant relationships. The beginning of a thing is important and shapes the entire existence of a thing. The saying, "It is not how you start, but how you finish", is not always correct and I can prove it.

A structure that begins with a faulty foundation is always at risk because it is not built on something solid. If an organization is constructed on or modeled after demonic principles, then that organization is demonic, regardless of the outward appearance of being good and sound. I say that to say everything that does good work may not be good. You cannot go on appearances. A tree can be beautiful, but if the roots are rotten, what good is the tree? How long will the tree last? God is pulling the veil off lies and deceit. Churches are being exposed so is it really so hard to believe that truth is coming forward regarding BGLO's.

My decision to renounce and denounce my membership was not based on the people or the good work that I know they do, but strictly on the foundation on which the organization was modeled and built. It began with freemasonry/masonic rituals which, if you do your research, will reveal it leads to Satan at the highest degrees.

You cannot hold a person responsible for what they do not know so I'm sharing what I have found. What I researched and discovered was there is an ancient Greek/Egyptian/Samarian/Babylonian, deity god or goddess associated with all BGLO and some are included in their rituals. Why? Because all Greek Letter Organizations (GLO) have a deity god or goddess associated with them.[27] Why does this matter? We know for certain GLO's are modeled after freemasonry and masonic practices.

In addition, Ancient Greek deities are the "men of renown", the nephilim discussed in Genesis 6. Nephilim are the children of a Fallen Angel and a woman. Why would we do anything in their name?

This next section varies depending on the organization. Each organization has a different ritual. During these rituals, initiates typically kneel at or around a table or assemble in a circle. This table may or may not have the Bible on it. It is dark, so candles are lit to create a dimly lit atmosphere. Here in the dark is where one takes oaths and vows to the respective organizations, in the name of the organization, and mentions or take oaths to the deities by invoking the use of their name. Depending on the organization's ritual, you may sign your name to a book, drink something, sing, or chant in the organization's name, which is all idolatry.

Unless you are an atheist/agnostic, this should concern you. When you are initiated, you do not have access to the rituals. You are so excited when it is time to go over. You are not thinking about what you are doing, despite being instructed to do so. In that moment we are placing our soul in jeopardy. We are making a covenant to generational evil and depending on the ritual intertwining by verbal covenant with the demonic realm. *Life and death are in the power of the tongue Proverbs 18:21.* The Bible tells us we are not dealing with normal fighting, but fiery darts and spiritual wickedness in high places.

> *For we wrestle not against flesh and blood, but against principalities, against powers, against the rulers of the darkness of this world, against spiritual wickedness in high places. Ephesians 6:12 and 16*

I struggled with discussing this at all because it is so ingrained, accepted, and revered in our culture. It is such an honor for our children to grow up and follow in our footsteps. We call them a legacy, but a legacy to what? I know this is difficult to hear, it was for me.

I am fully aware we have civil rights leaders, preachers, musical artists, entertainers, movie stars, athletes, politicians, doctors, lawyers, and all positions of affluence and respect who belong to these organizations.

Please hear my heart. My intent is not to cast judgment on anyone or the decisions you make in your life. If you choose to continue as you are, that is your decision to make. I hold no ill will toward anyone and will pray for everyone. I'm trying to inform people, who may not know or did not pay attention because it is so well hidden, albeit hidden in plain sight.

I won't delve any deeper. I may dedicate an entire volume to this topic. Also, I have respected friends, family, and clergy who are all members of these organizations, but I have a responsibility to sound the alarm as a watchman. Ezekiel 33:3. As I stated, all I'm offering is the truth. You are responsible for what you do with it now that you know.

Renouncement and Denouncement

My Brother and Sisters, please examine yourselves, talk to God, and do what God tells you to do. If you feel a tugging at your heart don't run away, that's the Holy Spirit. Continue having the conversation and ask God to reveal to you what you need to do. I promise you it is not a coincidence if you are reading this work.

This process of renouncement/denouncement has taught me so many things about spiritual warfare, demonic realms, spiritual wickedness in high places, and the power required to battle on this level. Now you may ask what level? When you decide to renounce/denounce secret organizations, there is a process required.

In this circumstance, renouncement was turning away from the organization and denouncement was pronouncing it as evil and repenting of my association with it. For clarification, what I pronounced as evil was the foundational origins of the Freemason ties.

I came across denouncement and renouncement prayers online and decided to use them as a guide for my prayers. It is important your prayers are authentic and speak your heart to God as you repent. What I wasn't prepared for was how many demonic entities I would repent for aligning myself with unknowingly. What scared me the most was the renouncement prayer for BGLO was one page, but the renouncement prayers for the Masonic and Eastern Star Orders were 13 pages long. There are levels in these orders and each level has a different demonic entity that is mentioned, and you have to free yourself from all those entities. The prayer takes time, but you will feel different when you are done. You will experience warfare because these entities do not want you free. The warfare confirmed this was real. At times you may even wonder if you're being dramatic and a fanatic. You are not. God will confirm that you are not, as He did with me.

Below is the link to the website, which contains the prayers and instructions to renounce/denounce all organizations, BGLO, Masonic, Shriners, Eastern Star, etc. I followed the steps after I went through the formal process with my organization.

www.outfromamongthem.com

Father God, in the name of Jesus, we come to you with a heart of praise and thanksgiving for the person who was brave enough to get to this point. Father God, I lift them up to you and I pray earnestly for my Brother or Sister who may read this work. Open their eyes to the truth. Heal their hearts when they see and believe the truth. Help them forgive themselves. Give them the strength to sever any ties or covenant bonds that may keep them from you. Hear their prayer when they reach out to you. I bind and destroy any demonic altar or mantle set up to keep them blind to the truth in this word in the name of Jesus, Yeshua the Christ. Meet them where they are, Jesus, and walk this out with them as you did with me. In the mighty name of Jesus, Yeshua the Christ's name. Amen.

NEW BOOK COMING SOON

Are you aware of the false reality you live in?

Do you want to learn the truth about it?

This book will reveal what you have been missing!

We live in a world in which enemies are everywhere, keeping us in a constant state of unknowing, where false reality is the weapon of choice that keeps us off balance and maintains the status quo. I was once like that, confused and frustrated about where life was leading me and it took a conversation with God to show me how to deal with these untruths.

With His direction I have come to understand many of the multiple mind-blowing revelations He gave me insight to and in this book, **Red Pill Revelations Vol 1: Know Your Enemy**, I will share them with you, so that you too can understand the enemy and his tactics.

By choosing the red pill you will learn truths about the false reality in which we live, one bitesize piece at a time, in a book detailing how you can prepare for what is out there and what is yet to come.

END NOTES

SECTION I-SPIRITUAL PARADIGM SHIFT

1. Paradigm shift Definition & Meaning - Merriam-Webster

2. https://www.tiktok.com/@unifyd_global/video/7313275789795953952?q=unified%20global&t=1705216020133

3. Michael R. Jones, "Apostasy," ed. Douglas Mangum et al., Lexham Theological Wordbook, Lexham Bible Reference Series (Bellingham, WA: Lexham Press, 2014)

4. Michael R. Jones, "Apostasy," ed. Douglas Mangum et al., Lexham Theological Wordbook, Lexham Bible Reference Series (Bellingham, WA: Lexham Press, 2014)

5. https://www.tiktok.com/@beauty_from_ashes7/video/7314288238221413674?q=demon%20erasers&t=1705216713239

6. https://dictionary.cambridge.org/us/dictionary/english/co-mingle

7. https://www.bibleref.com/Matthew/12/Matthew-12-45.html

8. Jackie Hill Perry (@jackiehillperryduh) | TikTok

SECTION II-THE SOURCE

9. Is Astrology A Sin? (with Video) Can Christians Believe in Zodiac Signs? | Christian Pure

10. Is Astrology A Sin? (with Video) Can Christians Believe in Zodiac Signs? | Christian Pure

11. What does the Bible say about astrology and the zodiac? Is astrology something a Christian should study? | GotQuestions.org

12. How the Meaning of the Word "Pagan" Changed (thoughtco.com)

13. What Is "Yuletide", Anyway? (historythings.com)

14. 13.What Is "Yuletide", Anyway? (historythings.com)

15. https://my.clevelandclinic.org/health/symptoms/21769-vertigo

16. https://writingexplained.org/renounce-vs-denounce-difference

17. https://writingexplained.org/renounce-vs-denounce-difference

SECTION III-THE SOURCE

18. What Is Time? A Simple Explanation (thoughtco.com)

19. What Is Time? A Simple Explanation (thoughtco.com)

20. What Is Time? A Simple Explanation (thoughtco.com)

21. What is God's relationship to time? | GotQuestions.org

22. As It Was in the Days of Noah | Renner Ministries

23. Religion in America: U.S. Religious Data, Demographics and Statistics | Pew Research Center

24. https://www.ccel.org/c/charles/otpseudepig/enoch/ENOCH_1.HTM

AN URGENT WAR CRY

25. https://www.youtube.com/watch?v=8oRRZiRQxTs

26. Greek Life (outfromamongthem.com)

27. Every Greek House Has A God Or Goddess (theodysseyonline.com)

BIBLE REFERENCES

1. (2023). Bible Hub: Search, Read, Study the Bible in Many Languages. https://mail.biblehub.com/

2. (2023). BibleGateway.com: A searchable online Bible in over 150 versions and 50 languages. https://www.biblegateway.com/

3. (2023). biblestudytools.com. https://www.biblestudytools.com/

4. (2023). OFFICIAL KING JAMES BIBLE ONLINE. https://www.kingjamesbibleonline.org/

5. (2023). YouVersion | The Bible App | Bible.com. https://www.bible.com/

REFERENCES

Admin. (2016, July 18). *Renounce vs. denounce: What's the difference?* Writing Explained. https://writingexplained.org/renounce-vs-denounce-difference

As it was in the days of Noah. (2023, October 3). Renner Ministries. https://renner.org/article/as-it-was-in-the-days-of-noah/

(2023). Bible Hub: Search, Read, Study the Bible in Many Languages. https://biblehub.com/

(2023). BibleGateway.com: A searchable online Bible in over 150 versions and 50 languages. https://www.biblegateway.com/

(2023). biblestudytools.com. https://www.biblestudytools.com/

The book of Enoch, section I. (n.d.). Home - Christian Classics Ethereal Library. https://www.ccel.org/c/charles/otpseudepig/enoch/ENOCH_1.HTM

Co-Mingle. (2023). Cambridge Dictionary | English Dictionary, Translations & Thesaurus. https://dictionary.cambridge.org/us/dictionary/english/co-mingle

Definition of paradigm shift. (2023, December 26). Merriam-Webster: America's Most Trusted Dictionary. https://www.merriam-webster.com/dictionary/paradigm%20shift

Is astrology a sin? (with video) can Christians believe in zodiac signs? (2024, January 17). Christian Power Tools For Living | Christian Pure. https://www.christianpure.com/learn/christian-zodiac-signs

Katt Williams Unleashed | Club Shay Shay [Katt Williams Interview with Shannon Sharpe]. (2024, January 4). YouTube. https://www.youtube.com/watch?v=8oRRZiRQxTs

Lundin, E. (2023, September 14). *What is "Yuletide", anyway?* History Things. https://historythings.com/what-is-yuletide-anyway/

Matthew 12:45. (2023). BibleRef.com. https://www.bibleref.com/Matthew/12/Matthew-12-45.html

The Odyssey Online. (2019, October 16). *Every Greek house has a god or goddess.* https://www.theodysseyonline.com/every-greek-house-god-goddess

Paganism definition. (n.d.). Bing. https://www.bing.com/search?q=-paganism+definition&form=ANNTH1&refig=f19960b-243ca499a9adc7fb60c7a5588&sp=2&lq=0&qs=LS&pq=pagan-ism&sk=LS1&sc=10-8&cvid=f19960b243ca499a9adc7fb60c7a5588

[@demonerasers]. *Predictive Programming & Demonic Prophecy.* (2023, December 18). TikTok - Make Your Day. https://www.tiktok.com/@beauty_from_ashes7/video/7314288238221413674?q=demon%20erasers&t=1705216713239

Proverbs 14:12 - The wise woman. (2023). Bible Hub. https://biblehub.com/proverbs/14-12.htm

Religious landscape study. (2022, June 13). Pew Research Center's Religion & Public Life Project. https://www.pewresearch.org/religion/religious-landscape-study/

Resources | Out from among them. (2020). outfromamongthem. https://www.outfromamongthem.com/resources

Secular. (2024). Cambridge Dictionary | English Dictionary, Translations & Thesaurus. https://dictionary.cambridge.org/us/dictionary/english/secular

Unifyd Global. (2023, December 16). *Laura Aboli Transhumanism: The End Gane* [Laura Aboli Speech]. TikTok. https://www.tiktok.com/@unifyd_global/video/7313275789795953952?q=unified%20global&t=1705216020133

Vertigo: Regaining your balance. (2023). Cleveland Clinic. https://my.clevelandclinic.org/health/symptoms/21769-vertigo

What is god's relationship to time? (n.d.). GotQuestions.org. https://www.gotquestions.org/God-time.html

What is time? Here's a simple explanation. (2017, December 29). ThoughtCo. https://www.thoughtco.com/what-is-time-4156799#SnippetTab

Worldly. (2023). Cambridge Dictionary | English Dictionary, Translations & Thesaurus. https://dictionary.cambridge.org/us/dictionary/english/worldly

www.ingramcontent.com/pod-product-compliance
Lightning Source LLC
Chambersburg PA
CBHW062113290426
44110CB00023B/2802